Electricity

Hugh Westrup

Consultants

Pearl Tesler
Physics Instructor
City College of San Francisco

Paul Kostek
Principal, Air Direct Solutions,
Seattle

Michael Patterson
Principal Systems Engineer

Publishing Credits

Rachelle Cracchiolo, M.S.Ed., *Publisher*
Conni Medina, M.A.Ed., *Managing Editor*
Diana Kenney, M.A.Ed., NBCT, *Senior Editor*
Dona Herweck Rice, *Series Developer*
Robin Erickson, *Multimedia Designer*
Timothy Bradley, *Illustrator*

Image Credits: Cover, p.1 Shutterstock; p.6 Album /
Prisma / Newscom; p.9 ArSciMed / Science Source; p.7
David Sanger Photography / Alamy; p.25 George Grall /
National Geographic Creative; pp.4, 5, 8, 9, 11, 13, 17, 21,
24, 30, 32 iStock; pp.28, 29 Janelle Bell-Martin; p.7 Mary
Evans Picture Library / Alamy; p.21 Timothy J. Bradley;
pp.23, 27 Wikimedia Commons all other images from
Shutterstock.

Library of Congress Cataloging-in-Publication Data

Westrup, Hugh, author.
   Electricity / Hugh Westrup.
        pages cm
   Summary: "Computers, refrigerators, and lights. They
are all powered by electricity. Many everyday objects
need electricity. But what exactly is it and how does
it work? Dig deeper into understanding the beautiful
mystery of electricity"-- Provided by publisher.
   Audience: Grades 4-6.
   Includes index.
   ISBN 978-1-4807-4681-7 (pbk.)
1. Electricity--Juvenile literature. 2. Electric power-
-Juvenile literature. 3. Electricity--History--Juvenile
literature. I. Title.
   QC527.2.W47 2016
   537--dc23
                                        2014045204

Teacher Created Materials
5301 Oceanus Drive
Huntington Beach, CA 92649-1030
http://www.tcmpub.com

ISBN 978-1-4807-4681-7

Table of Contents

Power Hungry 4

Early Studies 6

Electrons on the Move 8

Controlling the Current 14

Electric Glow 26

Think Like a Scientist 28

Glossary 30

Index 31

Your Turn! 32

Power Hungry

The date was August 14, 2003. The time was late afternoon. A large part of eastern North America lost power. More than 50 million people had no electricity. Cell phone service went down. Traffic lights failed. Trains and subways stopped in their tracks. Service stations couldn't pump gas. Businesses had to close.

Nightfall brought more troubles. Refrigerated food started to spoil. People had to use candles and flashlights to see in the dark. Stranded workers had to sleep on park benches. Miners were trapped below ground all night.

Before

Most power was restored within two days. But the blackout reminded people how much modern life needs electrical energy. Almost everything we do requires electricity. We need it to travel. We need it to communicate. We need it for cooking, heating, and lighting.

But what is electricity?

After

Early Studies

It wasn't always clear what electricity was or what caused it.

Thales (THEY-leez) was the first scientist to study this great **force**. He lived more than 2,500 years ago in Greece. Thales worked with pieces of amber. Amber is a hard, golden resin found in trees. Thales rubbed the amber with a cloth. That gave it the power to attract bits of straw. These were early studies of static electricity. Thales didn't know what was going on, but he saw its power.

In 1820, scientist Hans Christian Oersted found that a magnetic needle lined up with an electrified wire. The relationship between magnetism and electricity wasn't clear. But it appeared the **current** in the wire was acting on the needle even though they weren't touching. In 1831, Michael Faraday proved that moving a magnet through a loop of wire made an electric **field**. The wire became electrified.

Scientists knew they were on to something even if they didn't know what it was yet. Finally in the 1860s, James Clerk Maxwell showed how electricity and magnetism were connected. And the world was electrified with new ideas!

Hans Christian Oersted demonstrates a needle's reaction to an electrified wire.

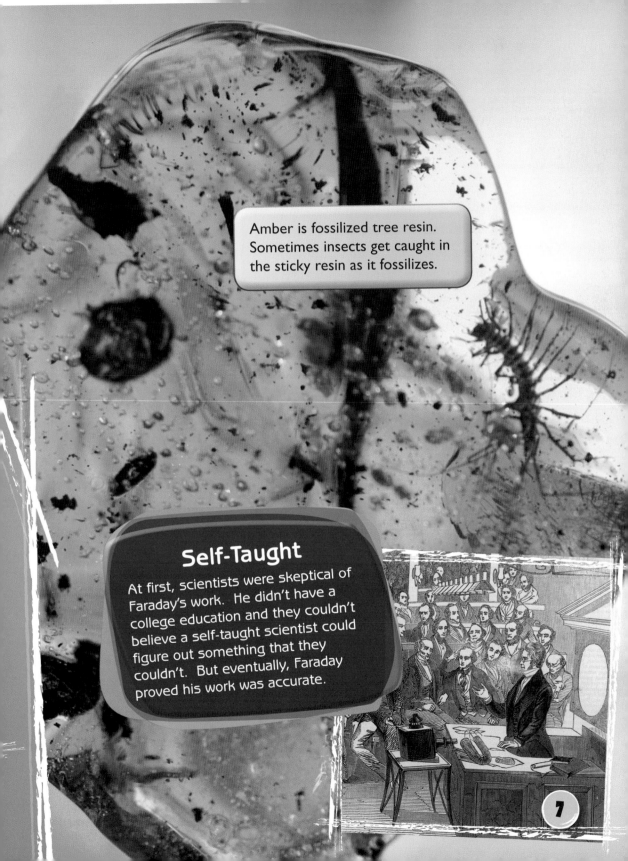

Amber is fossilized tree resin. Sometimes insects get caught in the sticky resin as it fossilizes.

Self-Taught

At first, scientists were skeptical of Faraday's work. He didn't have a college education and they couldn't believe a self-taught scientist could figure out something that they couldn't. But eventually, Faraday proved his work was accurate.

Electrons on the Move

Electricity is still fascinating scientists two thousand years after Thales. But today, it is better understood. All matter is made up of particles called *atoms*. Atoms make up everything from our ears to the air we breathe. They're very small. Billions of atoms can fit on the period at the end of this sentence.

It was once thought that an atom is the smallest thing there is. In fact, the word *atom* comes from the Greek word *atomos*, which means "indivisible." The truth is that each atom can be divided. It's made up of smaller parts called *protons, neutrons*, and **electrons**. The protons and neutrons form the nucleus at the center of the atom. Electrons are smaller and lighter. They move randomly around the nucleus in sections called **orbitals**.

Protons have a positive charge. Electrons have a negative charge. Neutrons have no charge. Most atoms have the same number of protons and electrons. An atom of sulfur has 16 of each. An atom of copper has 29 of each. An atom of silver has 47 of each. The equal numbers balance the charges. The negative and positive charges are the same. So, the atom has a neutral charge.

But sometimes, that balance is upset. And that's when electricity is created!

Smaller and Smaller

Today, scientists know that the atom is not the smallest piece of matter and can be divided. They are still searching for the smallest piece of matter. Some scientists think matter can be infinitely divided. That means you can keep splitting matter forever.

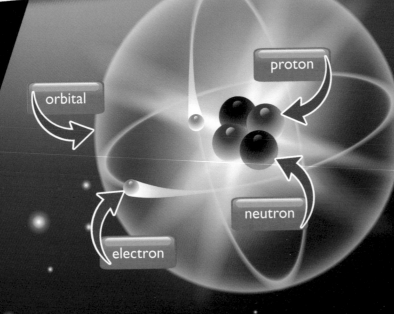

orbital

proton

electron

neutron

Quirky Quarks

Quarks are particles that have only a part of a charge. They combine in groups to make up protons and neutrons. There are six different types of quarks: *up, down, strange, charm, bottom,* and *top*.

Electrons are active particles. They can jump from one atom to another. They can even leap from one object to another. Sometimes, the atoms in one object lose electrons. Then, that object has a positive charge. The other object gains electrons. It develops a negative charge. Static electricity is the resulting buildup of a charge in an object.

When the flow of electrons is constant, it creates a current. This is what we use to power our world. You can picture it like water flowing. Long ago, we used water to power machines and do different types of work. Today, we just flip a switch. We use electricity to power our TVs, tools, and more.

Moving water, just like electricity, has two **properties**: **pressure** and flow. A fire hose can shoot water at high speeds. Intense pressure moves the water. A drinking fountain has low pressure. In electricity, **voltage** is the pressure. It pushes an electric current through a wire. In

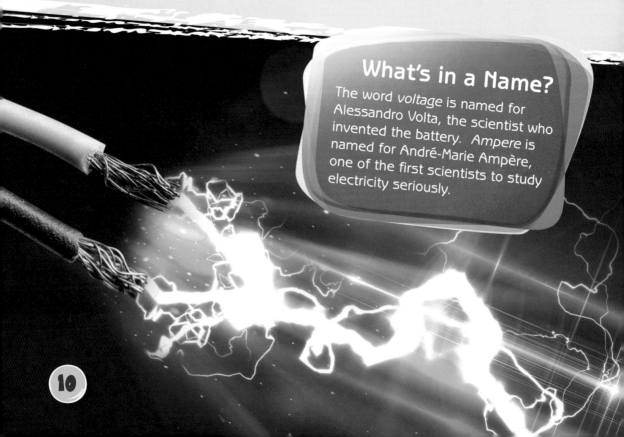

What's in a Name?
The word *voltage* is named for Alessandro Volta, the scientist who invented the battery. *Ampere* is named for André-Marie Ampère, one of the first scientists to study electricity seriously.

a hose, water moves from areas of high pressure to areas of low pressure. In electricity, electrons move between areas of different electric charges. A high voltage means electrons are jumping more often between atoms.

The flow of water is the amount coming out of the drinking fountain or hose. Flow is also a property of electricity. In electricity, flow is measured in **amperes** (amps). This is the number of electrons flowing past a point per second. A strong flow of electrons results in a strong current. Zap!

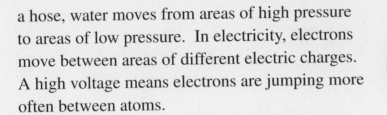

Electricity flows like water from a hose or a faucet. It has pressure and flow.

The electrical power of an object is measured by multiplying voltage and amps. Higher voltage and more amps means more power. Electrical power is measured in **watts**. A watt is the rate of energy transferred, generated, or consumed. In other words, it shows how much power is needed to run something or how much power can be made.

To find out how much power a toaster uses, multiply the power it uses by the time it's on. So if a 1,000-watt toaster is used for 1 hour, multiply 1,000 watts by 1 hour. Then, take a step back and look at the numbers. You wouldn't measure a football field in inches—yards make much more sense! In the same way, power isn't usually measured in watt-hours. Instead, it's measured in larger units called *kilowatt-hours*. (1,000 watt-hours = 1 kilowatt-hour). So, we divide by 1,000. That means that if a 1,000-watt toaster is on for one hour, then it uses 1 kilowatt-hour.

$$\frac{1{,}000 \text{ watts} \times 1 \text{ hour}}{1{,}000 \text{ watt hours}} = 1 \text{ kilowatt-hour}$$

Electricity from a lightning strike is enough to power the average home for a week.

Swimmers work hard to cut through water. They fight the resistance of the water. Likewise, electric current doesn't just run freely in wires. When current travels through wires, there is resistance. When resistance increases, current decreases. This decreases power. One way to increase current is to increase voltage. For instance, car companies can make electric cars go faster by increasing the voltage of the car's battery. This increases the car's power.

volts x amps = watts

Hamster Power

What can a generator do for you? A 16-year-old boy in England hooked up a hamster wheel to a small electric generator. When the boy's pet hamster ran in the wheel, the spinning motion turned the generator. The boy used the current to recharge his cell phone.

Controlling the Current

Electricity has the power to shock people. But it's really only useful if we can control it. Modern cities rely on a network of wires called an *electrical power grid*. The network carries current to the city. Electricity made by a power plant or a dam crosses the land in large power lines. Smaller lines branch off from the main lines. They carry the electricity above or below ground to buildings.

Dams and power plants produce currents up to 800,000 volts of electricity. But the electrical devices we use every day can't handle large voltages. A hair dryer only uses about 120 volts. Feeding it 800,000 volts would make it explode. So every electrical grid has transformers that "step down" an electric current. They reduce the voltage. A series of transformers steps down the voltage until it's suitable for daily use.

It's a powerful system!

Snap, Crackle, Pop

Have you ever heard a crackling sound or seen a blue light near a set of power lines? When there's moisture in the air, high-voltage power lines can produce a type of electrical spark.

Conductors

One way to control electricity is by carefully choosing the materials we use to build machines and appliances. Some materials can carry an electric current. Electrons jump easily between the atoms in these materials. These materials are called **conductors**. Metals are the most common conductors. Aluminum is a good conductor. Copper and silver are, too. That's why electrical wires are often made of long, thin strips of copper.

An electric current moves through a conductor in a chain reaction. An electron jumps from the first atom to the second atom. An electron from the second atom jumps to a third atom. An electron from the third atom jumps to a fourth atom. Zap! Zap! Zap! Zap! And on it goes.

copper wire

Direction of Current ⟶

free electron

Electrons jumping from atom to atom create a current.

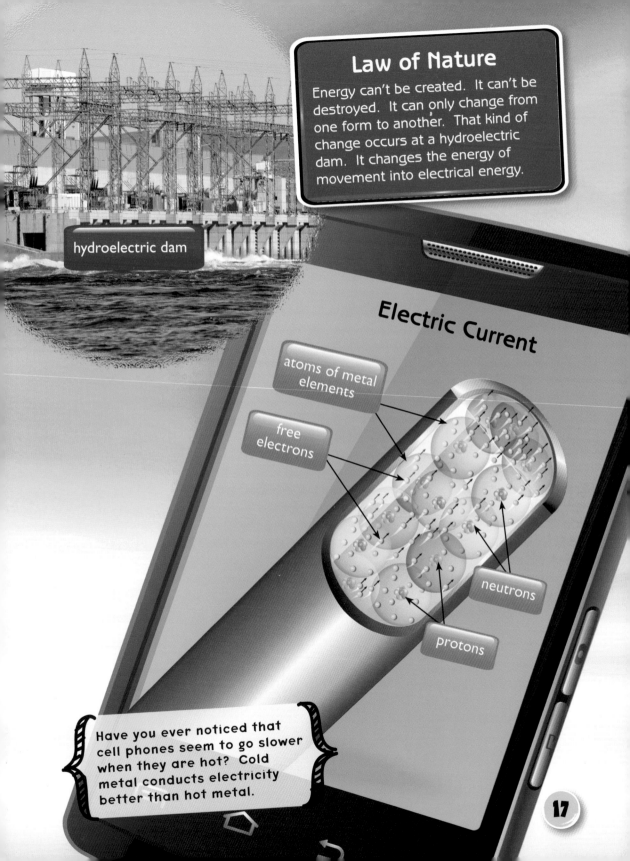

Law of Nature

Energy can't be created. It can't be destroyed. It can only change from one form to another. That kind of change occurs at a hydroelectric dam. It changes the energy of movement into electrical energy.

hydroelectric dam

Electric Current

atoms of metal elements

free electrons

neutrons

protons

Have you ever noticed that cell phones seem to go slower when they are hot? Cold metal conducts electricity better than hot metal.

Insulators

Some materials don't carry electric currents. Their atoms are not like the atoms in a conductor. They don't give up their electrons freely. A poor conductor is called an **insulator**. Wood, glass, paper, rubber, and plastic are all insulators.

Insulators are just as useful as conductors are. An electric current can be dangerous. It can shock you. It can even kill you. So electrical wires and devices are wrapped in insulators. They protect people from harm.

rubber insulator

Too Much Power!

No insulator is perfect. When super-high voltages are applied, an electrical breakdown can occur and an insulator can suddenly become a conductor. When this happens, there's a large jump in current and electricity arcs across the material. Lightning is a natural electric arc.

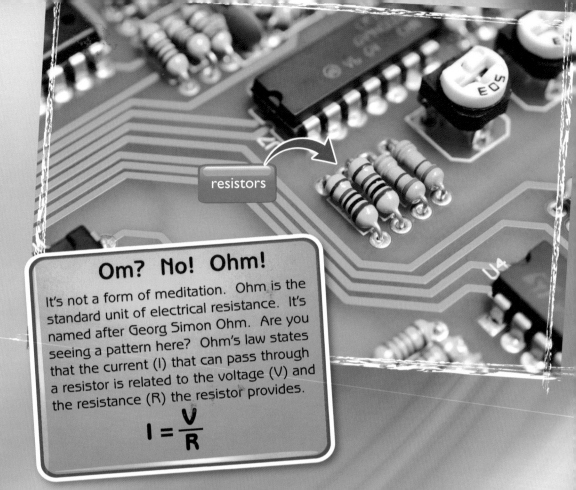

resistors

Om? No! Ohm!

It's not a form of meditation. Ohm is the standard unit of electrical resistance. It's named after Georg Simon Ohm. Are you seeing a pattern here? Ohm's law states that the current (I) that can pass through a resistor is related to the voltage (V) and the resistance (R) the resistor provides.

$$I = \frac{V}{R}$$

Resistors

Resistors are just what they sound like: materials that have high resistance to something else. Electrons move in resistors, but not as easily as they do in conductors. Resistors reduce the flow of current. They also lower voltage levels. They create resistance, just like what happens when currents run through wires…but more so! Some resistors stop large amounts of current, and others make small changes to an electrical grid. Resistors are an important part of any electrician's tool kit.

Circuits

Think of a model train set. Imagine it running 'round and 'round the track. Break the track, and the train stops. Electricity is like that train set. An electric current doesn't follow a straight path. It runs in a loop. That loop is called a **circuit**. Break the circuit, and the current stops.

Designing large and small circuits is another way to control electricity. Our electrified world is a series of circuits. Electric grids are giant circuits. They carry powerful currents from power plants to communities. Then, they return the current to the power plants. Your home is a network of smaller circuits. Plug a toaster into a wall socket. The wire between the socket and the toaster is really two wires in one. One wire carries an electric current from the socket to the toaster. The other wire carries current back to the socket. That completes the circuit.

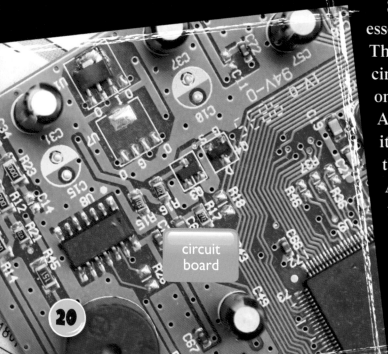

circuit board

Switches are an essential part of circuits. They make or break the circuits. When a switch is on, the circuit is complete. A current flows through it. When a switch is off, the circuit is incomplete. A current cannot flow through it.

Make Your Own

Want to make your own circuit? You don't need a fancy board to build it. Have an adult help you mix up two batches of dough—one salty and one sugary.

The salty dough conducts electricity. The sugary dough resists electricity. Connect them with wires, add a battery and a lightbulb, and you've got a circuit!

Salty Dough

Mix ingredients in a pot over medium heat. Once it forms a ball, knead it until it forms a dough.

- blue food coloring
- $\frac{1}{4}$ cup salt
- 1 Tbsp. vegetable oil
- 1 cup water
- $1\frac{1}{2}$ cups flour
- 3 Tbsp. cream of tartar

Sugary Dough

Set aside $\frac{1}{2}$ cup of flour. Mix the remaining dry ingredients and oil in a bowl. Slowly mix in the water. Knead the mixture until it forms a ball. Then, knead in the flour.

- red food coloring
- $\frac{1}{2}$ cup sugar
- 3 Tbsp. vegetable oil
- $\frac{1}{2}$ cup water
- $1\frac{1}{2}$ cups flour

Electricians must control two types of current. Remember Faraday? He found that moving a magnet near a wire created an electric field. It was the movement that was vital. As the magnet changes direction, the current also changes direction. It alternates back and forth, back and forth. This is what we call *alternating current (AC)*. It's the form used to bring power to houses.

Current changes direction at various frequencies. In the United States, AC power cycles 60 times per second. Other countries use different frequencies. Electricians like using AC because they can use high voltages with small currents. This reduces the amount of energy lost as current moves across power lines and into homes. And that's always a good idea—no matter which way the current is flowing!

Believe it or not, this is an image of city lights photographed at night over a long period of time. The dashed lines reveal these lights are powered by alternating current.

A Closer Look

AC power plugs connect computers, appliances, and other machines to alternating current in our homes. Different countries have different shapes, sizes, and types of connectors. All plugs have at least two prongs so electricity can flow in a loop.

Be safe. Never stick anything except a plug in an outlet. And be careful when you do that!

In a battery, electrical currents only flow in one direction. This is called *direct current*. Batteries are another way to control electricity. They power everything from watches to cell phones to laptop computers. Every year, we find new uses for them.

Alessandro Volta is the man behind the word *volt*. He found that an electric current can be made by chemical reactions. Soon, the first battery was invented. Batteries come in many shapes and sizes. A watch battery is small and round. A car battery is big and square. But every battery has the same basic design. At each end of the battery is a terminal. One terminal is negative. The other is positive. A chemical reaction at the negative terminal releases electrons. A chemical reaction at the positive terminal absorbs electrons.

Flashlights run on batteries. A wire runs from the battery to the lightbulb. Another wire runs from the lightbulb back to the battery. Turning on the switch completes the circuit. A current runs from the negative terminal to the lightbulb. From there, the current runs to the positive terminal. And then, it passes through the battery to the negative terminal. The bulb lights up. Shine on!

Recharge It!

All batteries run down. Their chemical reactions stop. But some batteries can be recharged. A current is run through them in the opposite direction. That reverses the chemical reactions. The batteries can then be used again.

Shock Tactic

Electric eels are predatory fish. They grow 8 feet long and live in the rivers of South America. Their bodies have thousands of cells that act like tiny batteries. Together those cells generate a current. It is strong enough to shock and kill small animals.

Electric Glow

Lights shine. Crosswalk signs blink. Buildings glow. Gazing out over the lights of New York City, some may see a beautiful skyline. But scientists see the magnificent flow of electrons. They see electric currents transferring energy, flowing over, under, and around us. Electrons light our streets, our cities, and our homes. They let us read late into the night and help us wake in the morning. Electrons power our world.

Electrified Earth

In 1899, Nikola Tesla used Earth's land and air to send 100 million volts of electric energy over 25 miles. He powered 200 lightbulbs at that distance with only one motor!

Nikola Tesla produces 7-meter (23-foot) arcs of electricity in his lab.

Think Like a Scientist

What does it feel like to complete an electrical circuit? Experiment and find out!

What to Get

- 18-gauge copper wire
- lemon
- ruler
- sandpaper
- steel paper clip
- wire clippers

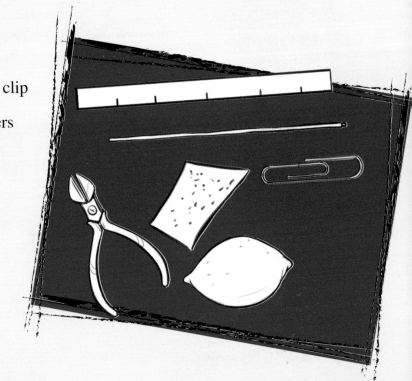

What to Do

1. Measure a 5-centimenter (2-inch) piece of wire. Cut it with the wire clippers. Use the wire clippers to carefully strip the insulation from the wire.

2. Unfold and straighten the paper clip. Measure a 5-cm (2-in.) piece of the straightened paper clip. Cut it with the wire clippers. Smooth rough edges off the ends of the wire and paper clip with the sandpaper.

3. Squeeze the lemon in your hand until it's soft.

4. Insert the wire and paper clip into the lemon. Position them so they are close to each other but are not touching.

5. Moisten your tongue with saliva. Pick up the lemon and touch the tip of your tongue to the free ends of the paper clip and the wire. What do you feel?

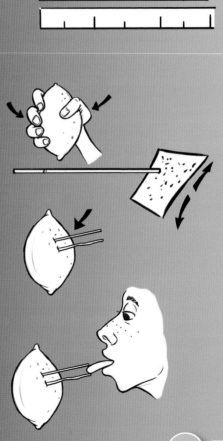

Glossary

amperes—units for measuring the rate at which electric current flows

circuit—a complete path that electric currents travel along

conductors—materials or objects that allow electricity or heat to move through them

current—a flow of electricity

electrons—negatively charged particles in an atom

field—a region or space in which an effect or force exists

force—a push or pull on an object

insulator—a material that allows little or no heat, electricity, or sound to go into or out of something

orbitals—regions around a nucleus in an atom or a molecule that can contain zero, one, or two electrons

pressure—the weight or force that is produced when something presses or pushes against something else

properties—special qualities or characteristics of something

resistors—devices that are used to control the flow of electricity in an electric circuit

voltage—the force of an electrical current that is measured in volts

watts—units for measuring electrical power

Index

amber, 6–7

Ampère, André-Marie, 10

atoms, 8–11, 16–18

battery, 10, 13, 21, 24

charge, 8–11

circuits, 20–21, 24

conductors, 16, 18–19

electric eels , 25

electrons, 8–11, 16–19, 24, 26

Faraday, Michael, 6–7, 22

generator, 13

grid, 14, 19–20

insulators, 18

lightning, 12, 18

magnet, 6, 22

Maxwell, James Clerk, 6

Oersted, Hans Christian, 6

Ohm, Georg Simon, 19

static electricity, 6, 10

switch, 10, 20, 24

Tesla, Nikola, 27

transformers, 14

Volta, Alessandro, 10, 24

voltage, 10–15, 18–19, 22

Giving Thanks

Take time to appreciate electricity with a fireside dinner! Grab some friends and an adult and try making a meal without using any electricity. That means no oven, no refrigerator, and no dishwasher! Talk about what you would miss most in a world without electricity, and enjoy your feast.